A MATTER OF
PERSPECTIVE

BLOOD WRITES OF PASSAGE

NATHANIEL NEW-CASTLE

Publisher's Note

Cover design by © DJMadameNoir
Edited by Paul Rogers

Published by Springer Literary House LLC
6260 Lavender Cloud Place, Las Vegas, NV 89122
www.springerliteraryhouse.com

ISBN Hardback 978-1-961078-77-2
ISBN Paperback 978-1-961078-78-9
ISBN eBook   978-1-961078-79-6

Printed in the United States of America

Message from the Author:

The poems in this collection were written over a period of about 13 years. Typically, the earliest poems are the most negative, thusly placed at the beginning. The most recent poems are the most positive. The poems were organised in a way to capture what you, the audience, see as you leap between perspectives, influenced by different emotions. This transition is reflective of my own journey from a darkened mindset to a more elated one; the places my mind wandered and the way I would look at things when feeling certain ways.

In the majority of these poems, the focus is on the imagery depicted, rather than the explicit meaning of the words used. This method of understanding is supposed to come naturally without focusing; if it doesn't, that's okay, not every poem can be understood by everyone at first glance.

If you don't understand a poem, you don't need to force it. Do, do not; it's all good. A general understanding of everything will weave itself together in time. No poem is written with the intention of being good or bad, they're simply written because the perspectives wanted out. No poem is about any specific, real person, no matter how it's worded.

"Amidst this battlefield I witnessed
What happens when darkness enters."
– N.N.Castle ~ Cadmean Victory

Special Thanks

(Names removed for anonymity, you know who you are):

To, of course, all friends and family that have supported me in the process of putting this collection together, thank you.

The decision to bring this book into existence came shortly after my grandparents mentioned that my sister enjoys my poetry. At the time, I had discarded poetry as a past hobby, left behind, and nothing more, with little interest to write anything. Hearing this invoked a call to action. To continue and make it something more significant, for the sake of a single fan at least. This has also led to a desire to take my writing more seriously and pursue publishing more work after this. Thank you, grandparents. Thank you, sister.

Mother helped me a great deal as I endeavoured to rework all my work, I received the best possible kind of feedback which was the kind that lacks a bias toward how I might feel from a mind that's capable of a deeper layer of thinking and understanding; a mind that can alter its 'perspective'. Raw, selfless criticism and brutal honesty demands the highest respect. Thank you, mother.

My wife allowed me to use her mind as a white board for my ideas and struggles. She is a key, consistent component of the support needed to keep me going. Always with comforting affirmations and reminders on what's most important. Thank you, wife.

The parent-in-laws often shared a deep interest in my creative exercises and expressed a level of engagement that kept me excited to show more to more people, pushing my drive to complete this project further than motive would have allowed otherwise. Thank you, mother and father-in-law.

All the encouraging words from long time and new friends. Specifically, from other Authors that I've been incredibly fortunate to not only come to know, but also who gave me their time, wisdom, and professional feedback. The assistance provided came in the form of deeper insight into the publication processes, marketing assistance, making my voice known in a podcast, creating absolutely spectacular art, massively editing every single poem with profound precision, and even allowing the opportunity for me to become an officially published author/poet by accepting my work in a collaborative anthology. Thank you, Randy Lacey, ML Wissing, Alfreed Fandangle, and Stephannie Rowe.

If I've forgotten anyone, just know it wasn't intentional.

Contents

Contents

Contents

Contents

Contents

The Suffering

I am content, there is no such thing as
    The suffering.

I am standing beneath two healthy trees in
    A field of broken glass.
Around me I see, off in the distance, that there are others
In a similar state as I, being sheltered by the shade of
    Two healthy trees.
My vision is broken, I cannot truly see
    The suffering.

I am standing beneath two healthy trees in
    A field of broken glass.
Around me rages the winds of torment, but my vision
Puts it to neglect, as I am sheltered by the shade of
    Two healthy trees.

I remain whole and unscarred while listening to
    The suffering.

I am sitting beneath two healthy trees in
    A field of broken glass.
Around me the winds have grown ever harsh.
    I am frightened
As my protection bends and groans; but still I am
    Sheltered by the shade of
    Two durable trees.

It's all around me, it's beginning to enter my mind
    As I listen closely to
    The suffering.

I am cuddling myself beneath two durable trees in
    A field of broken glass.
Around me are crashing branches breaking into shards of glass,
    Revealing spots
Of sunlight to light up my sight.
    I welcome the new warmth openly,
While I am still sheltered by the shade of
    Two breaking trees.

I have been offered warmth and clarity, as my eyes open to
    The suffering.

I hold on so tightly to my shade beneath two breaking trees in
    A field of broken glass.
I look out to others under the shade of their own
    Two healthy trees; and I am envious
As much as I am proud. They are so whole and perfect,
    But I have vision
And warmth while I am sheltered by the shade of
    Two breaking trees.

My eyes grow wider, there is balance as I continue
    To embrace the benefits of
    The suffering.

I am weeping beneath two breaking trees in
    A field of broken glass.

I am afraid. My conscious remains calm while
    My heart quickens the beat of its drum.
A devastating gust of wind sweeps the lasting serenity;
    One of the trees

Has completely fallen to its side, the other
    Losing half its branches,
Shattering in a million shards of razor-sharp glass.
    Sunbeams break through
Well over half of my shade as the foreign warmth
    Singes my skin and burns my eyes.
I turn and cower, deeper into the remaining shade of
    Two crumbling trees.

There is so much pain, I now see the origins of the glass,
    And I am overwhelmed.
But I have yet to succumb to
    The suffering.

I am in agony, there is so much to see
    And so much to feel
Even beneath the remains of the two crumbling trees in
    A field of broken glass.
I try so hard to avert my eyes, but curiosity
    Whips my vision
Like a slave to witness more of the truth,
    More to what plane of hell
I am hiding in, as a rodent would hide from an eagle.

I hold on with my dear life as the surviving tree
    Begins to bend
And creak under the forces of the Devils heavy panting.
    "What is happening?"
"Where did these viscous winds come from
    And why do they choose to haunt me so?"
My tears dry up instantly under the heat
    Of the sun's rays

And my muscles ache in attempt to hold up
    The source of shade from the
    Two dying trees.

Guilt settles in as I hit a level of awareness
    Highlighting my ignorance
Displayed in all this time I have spent without heat or clarity.
    I am falling with the final tree to
    The suffering.

This pain is immense, my eyes are scorching,
    And my skin reddens
And blisters while my body twists in torment
Beneath the presence of the two dying trees in
    A field of broken glass.
"When the trees whispered tales of the suffering,
    Is this what they meant?"

I cannot bear this; my blood is boiling with fear.
    Upon entering an endless repetition
Of seizures, my heart knows not, on how much more
    Of this it can endure.

My mind is analysing every detail,
    Making every second last
Twice as long, while it pieces together
    The reasoning for such cruelty.
With a final crash, the remaining tree
    Surrenders to the wicked winds
Of malevolence, and submits to its fate,
    By adding to the collection
Of razor-sharp shards of glass.

A Matter of Perspective

I can close my eyes and escape
    To shadows no longer;
The reality has revealed itself, and I
    Now bear witness
To what lay between me and the others
    In the shade of their own
    Two healthy trees in the distance.

I can now see that my anguish holds company.
    In the distance
Surrounding the others' two healthy trees,
    Are an infinite heap of suffering souls;
All marching, all burning beneath the sun's
    Furious clarity.

I am now left burning without the shade of the
    Two shattered trees.

A final fit, and I stand to my feet; I begin walking.
    I am surrendering to
    The suffering.

I now walk the endless planes of pain without the shade
    Of the two shattered trees in
    A field of broken glass.
I realise my heart still pumps blood,
    And I make a most selfless decision.
Halting my progress to nowhere,
    I place my hands upon my knees.

With an unsettling presence of peace,
    My stomach shreds, allowing blood to fill its contents.

With a single heave, I drain myself of blood as it pours
    Through my mouth.

While my blood is exposed to the sun,
    It dries and solidifies,
    Becoming as solid as diamond.

Half of me is drained of what life I have left,
    And I pause to regain
A minuscule amount of strength; in a second heave,
    I drain myself
Entirely of blood. I straighten myself back up,
    And slowly walk away

Leaving two short crimson pillars of solid blood behind me;
    To resemble how
I have so willingly given up my life in order to feel no more.
    My body is left
As a stiff shell filled with nothing but despair,
    Although my heart still pumps
A few drops of blood. "How is this so?"

My eyes have been drained of all fluids,
    And I am finally able to forever hide in darkness.
Without the sufficient flow of blood,
    My mouth is left wide open
To resemble the knowledge I own of the horrors
    That surround us all.

My skin is dry and charred as black as the Devils heart
    That has sent me here,
To resemble how the sun's fires shall never haunt me again,
    For how can they,

When the damage has reached its peak severity
And is now my new standard? My mind has erased
    All memories

That of which I have survived, but I hold
    A newfound wisdom
With all the lessons I have learned
    In such a small amount of time.

I now walk with a steady, snail-like pace,
    Leaving my conscious
To ponder eternal nothingness without the shade of the
    Two healthy trees.

I will continue to hold onto what little drops of blood
    I have left, for hope that one day
They may be as seeds that grow into
    Two magnificent trees.

With this final thought, I continue my aimless wandering.
    I remain a survivor; of
    The suffering.

But the cost...

Futile

Stop talking!
Your skin is blistering.
In your veins
Frustration seeps,
You're failing at bleeding
Clear melodies,
Lessons for the weeping.

There is something
You're forgetting,
Your purpose on Earth
Is to be a helpful being,
With clear insight,
Giving others clarity,
But your heart is rotting.

You're sobbing,
You're breaking,
You're wailing;
Flailing your arms

For help, you're calling,
Crawling,
Slowly
Dying.

You're dead,
You have failed your duty.
You are nothing,
Nothing are you.
Loneliness is what's coming
And there's nothing you can
Do.

Forever swimming
Until the abyss
Is all that's left to choose.
Forever drowning
As you're pulled under,
Wrapped entirely by the gloom.

A Family

A family torn to pieces
Leaves those inflicted
With bitter traces,
With the carcasses
Of forgotten memories,
Of discarded trust
And hopefulness.

Scars are formed
With an evil grope,
A loss of hope
When we cut the rope.
Melodies are losing
Their magical notes.

A family is an orchestra;
Some consist of flutes,
For the touches that come
Softer; rougher are
The drummers; violinists
Come in so sweet;
And for the oddity
Of the family,

A bass guitarist,
Playing his heaviest.
They all have their
Own ideas of how
The music should sound,
But together they all

Play along
In the middle ground.
A family that splits when
The music is lost,
When blood comes
As the greatest loss,
Pouring, 'til it slows to drips.
Some may move on,
But not all are that strong.

The flautist is left playing alone,
Playing their song
While the others find
New instruments,
Leaving their old ones, gone.

A family of some kind
Is what we all need.
We need others to fit
In relation to our mind.
You can even be
Your own family
If you wish, but all in all,

We need company to strive
And to fight the demons
That hide. For a soul
With naught only but
Their own song?
An idle soldier against
A thousand-armed strong.

Irreparable

At the bottom of my foot
Was the tiniest of cuts.
I never even noticed
The push, the prick
That pierced
Because it could.

So now, such time
Has passed,
I'm all dried up
And completely drained
Of blood,
With only seconds
Left to last,
And I feel my breath
Escaping too fast.

From a cut
Lead to the drugs;
Too much
Wasn't ever enough.
Until one day,
Too much
Finally caught up.
Dreams of
A broken escape

Break the heart
Of the living.
And The Taking
Cannot stand
The site of weltering,
They cannot stand
The sight
Of their own
Evil doing.

Swallowed Lament

Silence brings the tormented,
The quivering, and augmented,
And undeserving of penitence;
A quiet breath brings in the dead.

We're swallowed whole
By the depths of Sheol,
As we lock away our souls
To turn as black as coal.

Smothered in fiery water
And bloodied sawdust,
This is the gore house
That will forever haunt us.

And I'm watching you watch me
As I stutter and I fail to scream
The reason we should let them be,
The reason we should be let free.

Unduly Dormant

It was young, at its peak, until its demise.
Further, a veiling by, unspeakable truths,
Pitched as strengths to conceal broken ties
Brought a type of self-destructive abuse.

Although dead, it never truly fades away.
Consciously, patiently, it hides and waits.
Deep down, it's sleeping, mouth agape,
Jarred in place; torment with no escape.

Unknowingly, this beast was a protector.
Without its cruelty, a heart is kept sombre.
While the beast remains in its slumber,
There is no will to fight, nothing to remember.

Scars

Another
To stop the emotion flowing.
Another
To bring the heart rate rising.
Another
To stop the anger fuming.
Another
To halt the wicked looming.
Another hack…
Another slash…
Another to bring it all back…
Another to help distract…
… Another to fade this world
To black…

Silhouette in the Mirror

Silhouette in the mirror,
Answer me my screams!
A fellowship brings
The gold, the silver.
What does this mean?
What am I seeing,
While you wash
Away your dreams?

Silhouette in the mirror,
Answer me my pleas!
I see fire in my streams
And I'm afraid to face
The reflective flames,
For all wounds that bleed.
There's so much blood
To see; too much
For reason to perceive.
Not even the beast
Sits still in his seat
When there's so much
Bloodshed to greet.

Silhouette in the mirror,
What has befallen you?
I see your wrists
Dripping blue,
The sight chills my
Bones right through,
But I can't look away;
Not now, not ever;
For, I think I'm in love
With your gloom.

Silhouette in the mirror,
I know the silence
You choose, and I
Am afraid I must give you
My noose. Hush
Your fear, for once
You fall, no life,
Will anyone lose,
For all of your
Knowledge and clues
Have been written away
For others to view.

Entity of Dark

Not a godlike entity, just the universe
Giving back what it stole. Emptiness
Filled with something wholly mystifying,
Cursed as nothing, without the soul
Of another. While consumed, I,
In-turn, consumed the dead;
And the dead consumes all but de-
-Pravity, and in this riddle, we
Find the monstrosity; all that
Returned was a mutilated copy.
Imprisoning others in its own distress,
Clipping feathers, and laying them to rest.
Cloaked by the light, as if it was blessed.
Instead, a demon of the night to detest.
Convulsive tears, pillaging their interests,
Collecting their fears, and leaving a mess.
This is the Dark Wolf, whose timidness
Will leave you deceived; the Dark Wolf,
Whose existence is not at all what you believe.

Where Future Blights

Where were we when we met in the night?
Why didn't we see the beast that resides
In each of our eyes? We set out to squander,
To plunder the soul of wonder, forever,
For everyone leaves, dies. For this torture,
I don't know how to read why, or if I'd
Ever escape and find myself another.
A lover of gloom, bound to consume
You. Whilst everyone fights, dimming the lights,
There isn't any difference, with no insight;
No leverage to lessen the burden, the strife.
No lessons taught to prevent future blights.

You Shoe-ly See

I see you looking right through;
And I can't help but choose
To feel the sadness in your shoes.
Clues bring your past into
A view so vast; I knew
Your love would never last.
So now, you walk
On shattered glass,
And the pain in my feet
Is way too harsh.
Walk straight to what you can,
This is the only use we hand to
Our fancy, golden shoes.

Subjugation

Your collection of blood drenched whips,
A clear-cut testament to your sick mind-tricks.
Control was only gained by tearing at the seams.
So overworked, creating rips for expansion by ships;
Or in other words, for invasion after the long trip.

Taking away what others sip, some time lapses,
And now we're flying over to gun them down by the hip.
We're playing the same games as we have for generations,
Only with different words to phrase, and different elements
To manipulate. Everything has a price to pay;

Another's life can be saved, only by throwing yours away.
You may act proud and stand tall, this doesn't mean
You stand without shame. Even if you shut your eyes,
Your demons will still look you in the face.
They're still standing firmly in their place,
While you close your mind, and try to control an entire race.

Not a Care

Fire your detrimental gun
Through the lifeless hung,
Killing the dead with
The praise of your tongue
And rotting the beds
Of children so young.
This is the worth
We now put to birth.
Glorious is our world;
To celebrate, we burn.
Our mother's screams
Shan't be heard, for we
Are also far too busy
Dismembering our concern.

Power and Fear

"Please! I request aid, some benevolent help!"
My silence is broken, but only by a shallow yelp.

Forever locked in this despicable spell,
Of what some may claim as intelligent clarity.

Sure, through everything, it is possible I see glory,
But so, I also look directly at everyone's tears in hell.
Over there, 'she' fell and now 'his' heart melts.
It's typical of us all to rely on a miracle, something magical...

To be the next big thing, completely and utterly radical.
To walk in these charred and blackened halls
Appears to me to be everyone's goal, upon which,
With every single step, hardens and darkens their shell,

But the harder and darker they get, the more pressure,
That never lessens, on their soul. The soles of their shoes
Are forming burning holes. Why must they persist
And walk on scalding coals? With shivering, frosted, cold

Shoulders, we're a variety of mixed emotions. This cycle,
This profound rotation, is a mix of temperatures
Influencing illusions. There is so much of this unruly
Commotion, and it seems, no one wants it sorted.

They're persistent on making life itself, to be disputed.
If life is something to be controlled, who decided?
No names provided, no blame to be given.
It so often appears to me, that we are driven

By a singular purpose, by one simple reason.
It's like everyone just wants unlimited power,
And to be in the leading, highest-ranking position.
Should you reap them of this aspiration?

You would also witness the world thrown into
An endless, insufferable depression, because
They can't face the fact that, in the entirety
Of the universe, we're helpless men.

Afraid of the day they repent. Afraid to face
What's left to mend in the hearts they bent.
Afraid of losing their only friend in the end.
Afraid of the unrelenting demons they sent.

Narcissist

Picture your pouring blood if I
Were to slice off your tongue,
Throw it to the mud where
The tasteless ones run.

Picture your gushing blood
Running off into the fog.
The teeth break, that dealt wrong;
Now left to bites from black dogs.

No Room Ever Again

In these walls
I crawl, and I crawl.
Down these halls,
I watch their blood fall.
Lurking in the shadows,
Evasive of rotting gallows.
Plotting against their sorrows,
I hear them shout
For no tomorrow.
Without making sense,
We fight for old things kept.
Forget all past tense,
It's 'now' that's more immense.
But repeating this is to be more dense
Than those victims to this trench.
So instead;
In these walls,
I crawl without room to stretch.
Entitled to a nothing of a chore,
Nothing more than a rule of war.
Exhausted by the depth of a force
That's been scorned by your remorse.
Never again, to race into the rain,
To fill a face with the face of shame.
Less of the bloodshed. Now just instead
A haunting of a silhouette,
No less than what was never met.

My Apologies

And then it happened,
I'm sorry, I have failed.
My courage finally left.
And I'm swept in awe
Of others bravery,
Their ability to so easily leave
All their binding memories.
I still remain caught
In a spell. I am a leaf
Caught in the breeze.
I stopped reeling the well,
The bucket was halfway up
'Til the darkness, it fell.

I apologise for not being
What I needed to be,
For not nurturing
A shine in my eyes,
For exposing my cowardice.
I should never have taken
Off my disguise.
I ignored all the signs.
I predicted this day
Would surely come in time.

Truth comes in a rhythm
Of hypnotic chimes.
But when I told myself
That I'd be fine,
All I heard was
The hissing of lies.
I still feel other's
Hearts, but I
Can no longer feel mine.
I've given away
My final piece
To try and help others
Reach their prime.

Notice

I can't help but notice that the sadder I get,
The sadder you seem to me.
And I can't help but notice, the happier you get,
The happier I seem to be.
No, I can't help but notice, the more aware I get,
The more aware you are of we.
And I can't help but notice, the more you explore,
The more explorative I seem.
And I can't help but notice, the angrier I get,
The angrier you get with me.
And I can't help but notice, the more empathetic you get,
The more empathetically
I conclude, you and I are one, but I can't help but notice
I'm looking in a mirror
That is looking through me; because I can't help but notice
You not noticing me.

Poison Self

Scream for me all you wish;
        I will remain shut.
Please don't take this harshly,
        It's just
My company's been proven...
        As all too much.
My company's been proven
        To be the most...
            Potent venom.
It takes, but one sip
And you're...
        Incurably...
        Poisoned.

I know not where I am.
Walking in my sleep,
        To evade this vicious dream.
For I left my friend
        To decay in my cryptic den.
She's not of literal sense.
A metaphorical being
        For my ego, forever altering,
As a message to send
        Toward my wounds to mend.
A mind pried by 2AM.
Sinking in too deep,
        Swallowing dust just to bleed,
As I'm nothing now, again,
        But a shallow, colourless gem.

My Reflection

I knew a boy who was so strange,
Every day he always seemed to change.
I knew a girl who wore a mask,
She did so well to hide her past.
I befriended both, flipped their frowns;
Smiles for a while, all around.

I found out that the boy's mind was ill,
He had grown isolated and depressed.
I found that the girl was full of fear,
She was plagued by anxiety and distress.
I stood by, enjoying watching love start,
As the girl and the boy shared their hearts.

I discovered that the boy liked to hurt,
Scars amongst burns,
I discovered what the girl liked to learn,
Twisting and experimenting with limits.
I watched, dazed and confused;
No action to pull them from each other's abuse.

Until the boy, once again changed,
And the girl unlocked her entire past,
In all its horrifying unpleasantry.
This I didn't foresee.

The empty boy simply looked away,
With no emotion to track;
While the girl crumbled and screamed,
And sliced open his back.

Falling

I'm tired of grinding these letters,
These words, screaming out
In silent hurt to remind my heart
And mind to remain tethered,
Unfettered, and sane. Little
Did I know that you had already let go,
No, I never knew where these demons grew.

I'm tired of being quiet, no longer
Trying to hide it; where empty screams
Reside inside indifference; stronger,
I thought, in their silence. However,
Little did I know, you'd already let go.
So, then where have I fallen to, stuck in a loop,
I've yet to land at the tree's roots.

A Matter of Perspective

Old for New for Old

How could you see me hiding,
Biting behind my teeth?
We changed, got rearranged,
But for the better at least;
I think…

A touch lost contact, can't reach
You, to polish away the rust.
Never must we mourn the cost
Of love, and broken trust;
On the brink…

The usual business of reincarnations,
New blooms amongst scattered thorns,
Stab-back at bellowing horns that cry
Brighter than a thousand weeping dawns.
Bury them deep, and revive the fights
From previous lives that started it all.

Eyes Bleeding

It was nothing that could ever last,
Only start, with a simple spark,
A fire to burn the inside of your heart.

You always knew he would play his part
In making such a scorched mark.
Hark not, what was destined to rot.

Scandalous in his devious plots,
To bring about broken things lost,
In a plane, so opposite of something soft.

So, cradle the Raven curled in your hair,
Mimic his wicked, hollow glare,
With the rest of the world to share.

See her when she's never there.
Her eyes, of a Raven; unshaven,
Unridden of the hopelessness given.

Forever her own companion,
Blood lust now neglects her applicants
To be her devoted advocates.

The Final Empty Screams

How do I say it?
What am I to tell?
My silence is broken,
Only by more of the unspoken.
By wielding the dagger of darkness,
That keeps my screams empty,
I giggle under the fire's surveillance,
Fighting back its ethereal existence
And denying my mind
Of insidious intentions.

In spite of my attempts of release,
There is no shriek
That could pierce the bleak,
Shrivelled receipt
Listing all the fears
That be under my purchase.

I personally
Could not tell you what any of this means.
I just know
That when I think of the sunken whispers,
I feel as if emptiness
Is fighting with emptiness,
And that's all there is to be.

And the break that hurts the most
Is the one that occurs
When there are no pieces left
To be broken.

That's the break
We all so very much fear,
Because that's the break
That determines your direction
Forever until your journeys end.
Or so we think...

The Wing Wherewith We Fly

(Reference to: "Ignorance is the curse of God; knowledge is the wing wherewith we fly to heaven." William Shakespeare)

There is an infinite depth
Of intelligence; dive in,
You will swim through it.

With the journey begun,
The abyss fills your lungs;
Thrilling you with purpose.

Never to resurface.

A taste for knowledge
Ushers you to submit
Nothing quite as delicate.

Yet, so impenetrable;
Immeasurably so. So
Much; a quest to know

There are infinite answers
To whatever you crave;
Brave when persisting.

Never cease insisting.

You seek the blessings
Of knowledge consumed,
As you drown in doom.

Learn to breathe through
The tight squeezes,
Gets as hard as it pleases.

A mutual exchange of bitter-
sweets.

Amidst receding glee,
Its curse, could less care
For your desires laid bare.

For Better or Cursed

A tool, so insidious,
Slowly breaking beauty
Into something hideous.
It seems so ridiculous,
An ill found wish persists,
We see its existence.

Conjured through the mist,
And whipped back home
Are those trying to stay
Seated on their throne.
Their pride, a sword to hone,
As they beg another loan.

It may be a girl twirling
In her summer dress,
But even the innocent
Have so much to confess.
The notes and the numbers
That we possess, giving us
Naught, but greed to digest.

Bleeding like a struck pest,
Feeding the rest of us
With a little less feelings,
Look up to killer profits
As new gods to rid us
Of living distressed.

Little do we see, that
This poverty is breaking
The will of the hard-
Working, killing them dead
With hefty rents and debts,
Endlessly building egg-nests.

Good Work

Nice one Humanity!

Society seems convinced that happiness lies
At the bottom of a bottle,
In the destruction of innocence
Attending their first party.

Nice one humanity!

Forgetting to teach kids how
To use their minds properly.
No brain activity only conjures
Depression and anxiety.

Nice one humanity.

Forgetting to teach kids
That they have power, and thinking
Their only place is behind a leader,
Living like sheep.

Nice one… humanity.

Polluting young minds,
But not as much as we pollute nature.
We're a virus, we're a disease.

Nice one… "humanity."

We will destroy the land around us
To collect items that help us
Destroy ourselves.
It's an illusion that we're
Working toward
Any sense of serenity.

Nice one… "humanity!"

We manipulate each other,
Like we do our Earth.
Even fighting for a good cause
Pollutes it more.
We're biting the hands
that feeds, literally.

Nice one… "Humanity!"

We're words away from
Sending the bombs.
From bringing the humanity
Ending calamity.

Nice one… "HU-MAN-ITY!"

Mutilated

Engulfed by the fumes, and a black hole,
With no broom to hold on to.
I think the mushrooms loom too tall for us
In the darkness of our illuminated room.

Relevance is a trick of severance, takes away
The pain by stepping into the glade.
Ignore the storms and rain; eventually
You will bore of its taunts and rage,

As you will the pitiful restrictions placed
By those of age, the one's that strive to tame.
Which makes little to no sense; how can you tame
Anything of existence, when you're under its chains?

Any creator is not one to manipulate; you can
Only manipulate what's already been manipulated,
But even then, it's governed under a very different
Entitlement, for at that stage, it becomes mutilated.

Weave Ill

It's strange what drives you,
Far from a single weaved spell.
Regarding the benefit of others,
Undeniably, you strive to excel.
Regarding deeds by evil doers,
Undeniably, you strive to repel.

Unlocking locks of the lockers;
Those helpless, have within,
Long been locked, because
They know how it feels; the sin.

Empathetic, when a key is dropped
And lost, so, the motivation lies
Deep within, a smell of freedom
That sickens the sick, that bring
Webs to spin, driven by whip,
They begin to melt and drip.

The Old Scar

You're addicted and convicted
Of the heartlessness given.
So ridden with blood,
Lusciously driven from
The waters of the delivered.

Rendered immobile, after
An altered heart manipulated
Your nature, of being
So docile. And now?

Forever plagued by a
Fossil embedded deep
In your heart, without
Rescue from such trouble.

Sweet, Nothing

Craving your lips, as every thought
Traces back to your kiss.
Hands trembling over your hips;
With a smooth swish, your fringe
Is guided behind your ear's tip.
Eyes closed, our lips won't miss.

The fantasy follows as one;
Air whipped from our lungs,
Blood runs, as hearts beat
Like pounding drums,
Tendrils of lust stretching
To me and from you.

Until I realise, my mind is gone,
Broken back into reality.
You ask me, what's wrong?
Recollecting my fantasy,
I lie, and respond, "Nothing."

Empathy: Part One

I've got warm shivers watching you sink
To the bottom of other's rivers.
I can't bear to witness the devastation
You sit with, upon facing other's horrors.
And yet, here I am in your river, drowning
In your own horrors, wishing you would
Come back, to piece them all together.
And then I wonder, who is in my river?
But then I remember; I am the ocean,
The origin, that all rivers stem from.

Our Wasteland

A place of emptiness,
Void of emotion and soul;
A wasteland with less than
Enough room to crawl.

Where we grow to obsess,
And learn not to rest,
To adapt our eyes now
To this mirrored nest,
A place of emptiness.

Creatures with depression,
Dispersed amongst
The radiated worst,
Work harder, the harder
They burn; for this world
Knows no concern,
And cares less, for their curse.

Only through this test
Will they achieve, nothing
Less than a place
Of fulfilled emptiness.

Mussel

From the abyss of my emptiness,
It seems, nothing is forever.
Your piece of benevolence
And your entire summer,

A suffering brought only by
Myself to encumber
The serendipity of your
Own natural slumber.

Death be prior to
The place that I sliver,
To lie face-down at
The bottom of your river.

Consider, what not to be,
And how stronger I
Could achieve nothing
Less, than if I were weaker.

Leaking Canvases

My voice is less than a whisper.
I am without power… I wish!
I wish to make a sound to others,
But fate will not allow it.

I am drowned in my silence,
A penalty I must pay for
Trying to be the loudest,
Trying to be the hardest.

For shaming all those
Who were the kindest.

My mind, unclear as I hose
This sincere, white rose,
Lined with blood, a sacrifice
Was made, I suppose.

It's frozen, as she loathes
The stranger in the mud;
A wolf without his nose,
Unable to see what shone.

You and I, the most intricate
Painters shaping the flow
Of our souls, into these
Fragile, leaking canvases.

Parallel

Tiptoed to this new place,
With a new mask, a new face.
Left the dark without a trace,
Capturing the light in great haste.

You've made it to the house,
Made the putrid gleam-
On back, the match lit mouse;
Promised with an untouchable dream.

However; all that was unspoken
Was left for the broken,
Provoking the woken,
To kiss blood ridden lips, and
Grab their throat and choke 'em.

Forever; the guilt will be swept
Amongst the ages kept,
And the plague will be dreamt
Where the hallowed slept.

Humanity's Push

You were lured into the dark,
Wielding a blade to fight;
Why did you go and follow
What looked to be the light?

Stupidly, you thought
The choice was right;
Your vision was skewered,
A malevolent blight…

…Hones nothing but the putrid.

A quick glimpse at past times,
Shows the motion was fluent;
A gash, so slight, so bright,
Releasing precious fluids.

The scene is getting gruesome,
You're losing sight,
Lead here by sinister minds
And their ruthless cause.

It's too late now, to hear the chimes.

You were made so shy by
Those silly, wicked rumours.
You've ended your life now,
And that is not so humorous.

Deep Pressings

She's getting sick of her life.
Takes enjoyment out of
watching
Her own blood run from
The tip of her knife.

There is too much strife
Running through her mind.
Why is she left to be treated
This way by her own kind?

No one even helps at all,
To let her problems unwind.
She's constantly looking for
Happiness, but there is

Nothing she can find.
Through time, there is
A constant deterioration,
A loss of motivation;

There isn't a single station
Where she can rest,
To gather her thoughts
And her emotions.

She has lost it all,
Besides her devotion
To survive; she knows
She has to stay alive

In case she might find
Something that will
Re-spark her bright light.
Inside she knows,

Despite the logic,
There must be meaning
In her life, and she's right,
Quite a site, she will find,

With at least one other
Of her own kind.
One day she will
Finally make peace

With her vicious
State of mind.
Except, right now,
She's still running

Around blind.
"You'll be fine!"
She tells herself,
But her mental-health

Is driven further down
Where the lowest dwell.
It's obvious that she
Can't help herself.

Each time she reaches out
To someone else,
Her heart gets heated,
And melts; encased in

Her own cell, she is
The only one that can
Hear her shallow yells.
With all of this fear felt,

She now lacks the ability
To call for help.
Now, what would you do,
Oh listener, oh reader,

If I told you these feelings,
They don't just dwell in her?
There is a curse that has
Swept across the Earth;

Contagious as it leaps
Through a midnight whisper.
It must linger, even after
It's led someone to be

Strung up; strung out, in
Mysterious ways, leaves
Behind no lessons to teach
Of how to threaten

Its existence. The mere
Thought of its afflictions,
Are to be dreaded;
Lest we forget it.

Only a Feather

I'll do whatever to endeavour a fever;
But the pressure of a single feather
Quickly becomes a ton.
It quickly becomes too much
And grinds my bones to dust.

Straps of leather will hinder,
Even pulleys and levers will aid
The weights surrender;
But every foreign touch,
Every piece of broken trust
Lusts for my body to become
A bloody, gory, pile of muck.

Again

Again, my heart starts to simmer
As you look upon this killer.
Your eyes, to mine, they flicker;
Causes me to shiver, for I

Want nothing other than to be
The reason that they glimmer.
But I won't, I can't; nothing
Of the sort for me, ever lasts.

It comes and goes horribly fast,
With critical fractures and breaks,
My heart seeks refuge in a
Permanent cast, where it lies,

In an unbroken fast.
It will starve while outsiders
Cut themselves on my
Shards of broken glass.

Hardens, Tires, Hurts

I'm sorry for the neglect,
For cowering in the attempt,
To remain myself, content.

All I have for you is respect;
When you reveal your emotions
I feel all of your devotion.

You're a gift that God has sent,
But to you, I am the Devil's henchman,
Sent to leave you contorted and bent.

Every day, I feel such a great sense
Of regret. I repent that I will never be
What you need to mend your broken fence.

Forgive me for this stench; all I do is stress,
All I do is sweat. I try so hard to help you,
But I think I just contribute to your mess.

To you, I am nothing more than a threat.
You're growing closer, with every step,
To being blanketed by the most horrid of nets.

A net weaved by a soul depressed,
Adding an infinitely dense weight
Of dread on to your chest.

The day you leave, I'll understand.
I'm a solitary soul, that is destined to be
Kept company only by my companions

…That never tire of me.

Video games, music, books, and movies;
Drawing and food, With swinging moods;
And of course, my wretched poetry.

While I force myself to smile, to be happy
Occasionally. "Are you okay?" People ask me.
I respond, "Yes… it's just sometimes, I feel Lonely."

Corrosive Words

There's something eating me;
From the inside.
"Please, just don't even try."
And these words will burn my mind;
For all of time.

And who helps the helper?
A wounded pedlar with nothing to remember
Of the times he was aided by others.
Discouraged by a selfish favour
Enacted upon a selfless desire.
Not to speak of a sire;
A liar was never caught riddled in his own fire.
What of the situation to speak?

Nothing could be comprehended so bleak,
Pretentious in its attempts to remain meek.
Seek the silver tongue by the weltering tree
And maybe you'll have a service you seek;
For words abundant in abnormalities
Trick those poor, weak minds desiring to flee.

A great stimulation of the heart
Only caused by your mark.
I'm trapped in a love
That's as ferocious as a shark,
As lethal as a Poison Dart,

But the spark you've made
Is a bit of a pain;
Lain here
By an opportunities smear,
The destiny so clear.
But never shall it come near.
We're all eaten by our fears.
Forever, I'm riddled in your tears.

A Matter of Perspective

I Scream

Too broken to follow,
Rotting in the hollow,
Testing the shallows,
Sensitive to sorrows.
You sang without need,
Whilst I fought with greed,
And I wished you'd see
I struggled to be free.
I had you intervene when
The Devil I was to greet
Brought me to my knees,
Broke me; fate complete.
And now, for our final meet;
You jumped between me
And a crimson blade,
As I retreat, only to see
Your trampled body
By my horror's feet.
Apologies won't ever be seen.
Behind the darkest screen
You're gone, where I belong;
Where I cry and scream.

Demon's Debt

Piece together
The teeth of a feather
To endeavour the weather
Of a poor man's tether;
His tether to the nether,
His broken soul of a sinner.
There is no winner,
Only the survivor
That survives longer
Until a new record bearer.
So, forget this game
To win infinite fame.

So, forget this game,
Of humanities disgrace;
And forget the name
That brought us this face.
So many seem to detest
The words so remorsefully pressed
By a poet so horribly depressed
By the best of a Demon's debt.
She loves what you regret,
For no justification will be met
To justify what you spent
On the flower that crept.

Perjurer

These eyes are crying, so sad.
These lies are burning, so bad.
There is no justifying, no rad.
These acts, so horrifying, go mad.

Behind the deceiving and lying,
The tortured, forever dying
Under interrogation lights,
Too bright for fine dining.

Bring me these worms,
I'll see to their words
And so, I will ensure
They will no longer endure
The jaws of your Earth,
The taste of your cure.

An Evil Breeze

"Help me, I need a reason to breath."
I can't believe the blood I had to weave
To seize the song of those tortured leaves;
Besieged by this haunted breeze.
Those blown out, just to die
In the romanticised sky of the night
That strives, only to pry us from our lives.

Unseen

I never knew you, like I knew your truth.
Hiding inside those almost unseen eyes.
Drowning in your despise, I discretely spied,
That "Evil holds no excuse; empathy varies in fumes.
I'll die by tonight, be written-off from others' lives."

Existence is of little use, belligerence identifies
Your ruse, so obtuse, same rumours and lies.
Your hopes all held together by false highs.
Plastic lines up queues, wraps you into
The darkened views you choose of us.

I'm blinded by reason; you learn of all the various
Ways to live. I fight for you, my joy vicarious.

Vulture

With everything that could be,
It would not be understood; we,
Without a doubt, know that
It's not made for bad or good,

But for a scavenger on the prowl
Fighting amongst no crowd,
Taking on the remains from
Any and all battlegrounds.

Loneliness is a fickle feeling,
Fleeing to the skies, it flies
Free from its own demise,
Brings a macabre look to its eyes.

This bird became my distant watcher,
Following me down this acid river.
Forever, a glimpse of this lonely figure,
Will torment me, as I bend and shiver.

No wonder I am drawn to ponder
Upon its mystery, its features; to wonder
At the interpretable meaning of this
Tormented creature's hunger.

Fighting Hand

To watch you sink, shrink, shrivel,
While you bleed upon this seed,
Planted while you think about
What this beast requires of me.
To help your wrongs get right,
To help you win, to lend insight,
While you ride through life
Upon these holy mounts;
This blight has pushed these
Abilities of mine, to fight.

Beastly Games

He was a beast for you to tame.
Instead, you found a heart to raid.
A grade 'A' effort in taking out the prey,
A relationship that beholds shame.

Beheading the beast, exposed
Yourself to the bloody spray.
Devilish glares are thrown your way,
So, now what have you to say?

A cringing critter, so docile,
Not a beast that is hostile;
So, don't act like you were afraid.
Sing to the rain, all you wish,

But your praise will be unclaimed.
It'll take more than a spit-shine
To clean this wretched slate
Of the miserably betrayed.

A Sow's Silk Purse

Your lips' breath, silk,
And I, a scar
Upon the threshold of this
Crystal-lined forest
Of forgotten
Forever-promises.
A slave to the land's pests;
Rotten and grotesque.
My flesh is torn,
And drenched by my
Own blood, and that
Of the huntress.

She paces elegantly
With stress, allowing me
To reluctantly test
Her land-claim,
Her owned forest;
Meanwhile, ruthlessly
Killing the rest
Of my brothers
I knew best.
The hunter of the dark,
In this jagged forest,

Marked with mesmerizing stars,
Is somewhat of an evil plaque
Embedded within my own,
Stolen, broken heart.
So, the question I
Begin to ask; why
Do we take part
In this endless grey march,
That will only leave
You to starve?

I guess we all came
For something pure;
I guess, silk, be
The lure to an
Unfortunate thing
To discover; a never-ending
horror.

We Sync Weak Links

Surrender
To the forest;
Forever.
And the hands of these lovers
Meld into each-others.
Mixing their luscious colours,
They burn the ravens
By the hundreds.
Surrender
To the forest;
Forever.
"Break your chains!"
It's simple.
"Forget your pains!"
The request was to cut the strings
To what the darkness brings.
Sever ties with anything fragile,
Hold only to what's rationally tangible.
But never did I ever think
That strength would be the weak link.

Exit Ticket

If there was an exit, she
Would be completely
Obsessed, it's complex
At best, but lest she's told,
A secret nest could be
Something blessed.

Shivering in the cold
Core of a shipwreck,
She attempts something
Completely reckless;
She throws in the towel,
To digress, to point out
How it's all so worthless.

A decision considered,
A hearty consequence.
A pity she couldn't achieve
What was hardly believ-
Able, If only she knew
What was difficult
Was entirely possible.

In the end, probability
Was the least of her
Concerns, as eventually,
It was fear that brought
About her burns.
The eventuality, is she
Will become ethereal;

A dread, so unimaginable,
She will deny her body
Is physical. Serendipity
Is no option to be earned,
So, a heart will suffice
With a hard lesson learned.

Two Worlds of One

I'm a pawn to be torn
Between two worlds' scorn.
This isn't a fight to review
The biggest horns,
This is a stand for life.
Our customised strife,
That determines what we
See when we look into
Our eyes; good and bad,
Subjective to our own will;
To fight for what we have,
In order to justify our fill.

Leash No Life

On this leash, I'm a hound
Held down. On this leash,
Forever I'm drowned.
A circle is formed by my
Own body; deformed.
Around and around,
This leash keeps me bound.
Around and around,
A slow death, she knows,
Rewards no crown.
She finds it nothing
But selfish, spell bound.
A binding, only to perish.
A dog, forever proud
That its heart pounds.
A dog, forever proud;
Fighting the leash,
Until it found itself
Six feet underground.

Enduring

Just make it through another day.
Grades of grey blind and bind,
Paving the way with shattered clay.
Behind is an array of beautiful dismay.
Behind is so broken, it almost looks whole.
Behind cannot stray; must stay going…
Forward, is bloodied, with all shelter caved.
Forward is elusive, forward will betray.
Back and forth, I shift my gaze; either way,
I've lost it, thrown my soul away,
Just to make it through another day.

Clutter

An unbearable fight,
Just to take back what's mine.
I gave you my time,
Just for you to steal my mind.
So divided, and corrupt.
The end so abrupt,
But, you still own my
Heart and trust.

This time wasn't just lust,
It was a diamond embedded
Into the plains of Limbo's crust.
Faster and faster,
I endorse more disaster
By picking up a new,
And running the fine
Print right past her.

Hotter and hotter,
I scorch and boil-over
In attempt to forget
Our endeavours.
How can you forget
Something that was never.
You and I were never,
Never were we ever.

Although it never is as it was,
Something so immense,
Never will it be as it seems.
For it, to you, seems to not even be
Past tense, through your lens.
My words no longer
Even make sense,
And no doubt, in this poem,
I've made that evident.

As you read and
Scratch your head,
Trying to decipher
The clutter of this talk
Of things to dread,
Because, to you,
There wasn't ever
A single thread
Of sanity to be read.

Undeserved

It is commonly said that ignorance is bliss.
Uncommonly understood, is this;
That it's the killer of our innocence.
Lists of those being pissed on, grow
Further endless. While all of those
Who are charitably given a golden rose;
Loath the horrors of hauntings betrothed.

Forever Kept

Where did your heart go?
I don't even know.
It was suddenly missing,
And was ripped right
Out of my throat.
I was wishing in hope
For the living to end
This heartless suffering.
For there's something
That I've been remembering,
That part of you
That I miss kissing.
I'm singing with these birds,
While the raven pecks
My burns, and not a single
Piece of peace, nor hurt,
Could render the in-
Fluence of your words.
I won't ever attempt to
Forget you, and this will be
The reason; the four seasons
Still turn, so long as you
Remain in my mind,
Then I'll continue to
Press through time.

But I'll Forget

It's inspirational, nothing detrimental.
It's the rope that never sways,
A chain that never breaks.
It's music that only ever plays
When you stop, forget your way.
Nothing factual; yet not fictional
Until it's long forgotten.
       ... Slow ...
               Fast!
Smooth, with a hard iron cast,
Jagged with pearlescent shards.
Whatever the tempo,
It'll clench its fist hard,
Tightly around your tiny heart.
Forget your monotonous pace,
And bleed for these obscure cards,
Dealt by a tormented wind,
Blown somewhere from the past,
From somewhere long forgotten.

Alone

You're alone;
Sitting,
Listening
To music so fitting.
But you'll be alright;
Sitting,
Waiting
To start crying.
I feel your fight;
Sitting,
Clenching
Your chest that's burning.
It's such a sore sight;
Sitting,
Wishing
For your ending.
To see shadows, dim your light;
Sitting,
Reminiscing
On the old things.
I'll help you through this;
Sitting,
Realising
You decide on your placing.

Give a flick of your wrist;
Standing,
Grasping
A new understanding.
And wave away the mist;
Standing,
Smiling
At the greatness rising.
Kill off the abyss;
Standing,
Fighting
The darkness resisting.
But you missed;
Sitting,
Drowning
In others suffering.
You took a wrong turn;
Sitting,
Helping
Those receding.
What drives this new concern?
Sitting,
Drowning
In others torturing.
You're alone.

Lost

Leave. A concoction
Is brewing. The effects?
You wouldn't believe.
Sticky as sap from a tree,
No escape allowed.
It will take away
Your ability to breath.
So please, just leave.
I'm trapped, I need help.
It's an evident fact
That I've lost all trac-
Tion. I've been brought
Back to the faded
Realm of black,
With sanity snatched.
Again, I'm trapped.

Dim the Glow

Following the flow,
He allowed her to go,
To banish his glow;
If only he could know,
The glow is where
The bad ones go. Oh,
If only he would know,
That dimming the lights
Should some way prevent
Those horrid blows
That broke his poor
And weakened bones.

Lovable

You're likeable.
You're kissable.
You're huggable.
You're practical.
You're theoretical.
You're thoughtful.
You're advisable.
You're charitable.
You're delightful.
You're trustable.
You're respectable.
You're simply, magical.
None of that means
A thing to you.
You're not…
Lovable.

Forgetting Nothing

She's there, riddled, and she's scared;
Left to lessen her own stare.
It's the last dream of freedom and dare,
Cared by our wild, pitiful glares,
That would fend off the offending pair.
Our fear was thought as rare,
Merely temporarily in disbelief.
Were we ever to turn a new leaf,
We'd seek refuge in each other's dreams,
As it was bound by our demon's grief.
As teeth are naught without roots,
As orchards are pointless without fruit,
Streams of agony will be our seeds.

In hope, we grow in each other,
A mutually found place of peace
Within our twisted trees.
I'll never, for you, bring the decipher;
As you were but a dream,
And will never be as real as her.
Everything I felt was pain,
So, for you, I will have locked myself
Away in a place so far; in storms and rain.
A place guarded by a fiery glade.
When the smoke becomes plain,
It'll be the warning of you that I'd made;
It will remind me to walk the other way.

Fractured Reflection

A mirror of broken
Serenity displays
Only the evil things.

Cracks and fractures
     Are too easily seen,
        Despite

 Flawless glass
       Being
The majority.

My Silent Addiction

You don't even know
How impossible it is
To let go.

Each of your words follow
My own style
And flow.

Each of your words brings me
Such insidious hopes;
Endless sorrow.

You don't even know
How I desire to
Let go.

And, for each of your words
You slowly diminish
My glow.

Each of your words burns
Me horrifically
Slow.

You don't even know how
I loved you so; the way
I corrode.

Distracting Aid

The sound of your voice
Tramples out all other noise,
Like poison rising from
Beyond the void.

Trampling the sound
Of humanities ploy,
A desire to destroy;
You lock away its decoys.

These things labelled
As simple 'toys'.
I'm tired of this game,
So tired and afraid.

So, take my name,
Wash my wounds away,
For my sanity's sake,
For my fractured ruby's
replace.

Cliché

Oh, woe is me,
I will rain
Upon thee
With lines of heart,
With emotions of vague;
And
With words of cliché.
As I will pray,
For beneficial sake,
Thy will be okay.

That Week

For that week
I knew what silence was.
For that week
I wasn't fighting any wars.
For that week
I was following my own cause.
For that week
You weren't at all a thought.
Until the week ended;
Once again, you have me in a
haunt.

Whips of Knowledge

Mixing drips in this
Poultice of stripped,
Mangled flesh,
Deducted direct
From your ill-willed
Heart of iron mesh.
It only has me ponder
The usefulness
And relevance,
The impact that
Your existence
Claims to have,
On my happiness.
My conclusion?
That my time
Is priceless
And you are less
Than worthless
For guiding me
Directly to the abyss,
Of which only
Pestilence persists.
Although, to neglect
All of this as the
Biggest mistake,
From which comes
The greatest lessons.
Sure, I have learnt
A lot from these
Nine-tailed whips.

With or Without Passion

Certain foreseeable events
Will have led to concrete or
dread.
Cast in stone; invincible, but
Forever alone. It was said,
I couldn't forget unless I
Froze amid this emptiness.
Hollow, lest I may hold on
Tight to this thread. The looser
The grip, the harder it sets,
And the lesser the effort,
The harder it hits, but to
Hold on will let the passion
Seep through the slits.
A dire desire is the killer,
And my hands are charred
From nothing other than scars;
A lesson and a reminder.
Forever in demand of an
answer,
This conundrum has left a half
Body of stone. The other is in
Constant ignition of an
escaping fire.
To be overwhelmed by either,
Would mean to be blinded
By darkness in a passion fever.

Winter

This is a world so hollow,
And they'll curse those too mellow.
With devilish causes to follow,
What can one simple fellow
Do to simply let go?
My unknowing tomorrow
Will be your eternal sorrow.
By winter's haunts and hallow,
You'll never reach the shallows.

A Matter of Perspective

Drink

You wish for a drink?
A drink?
I guess I'll succumb,
And listen as my blood runs.

I'll hand you a drink,
It's exactly what you think.
My blood has spilled
To flow at your will.

I'll hand you a drink,
For destruction is at the brink.

Take this blood-filled cup,
It's bound to fill
Your charred,
Broken heart.

Take this blood-filled cup,
And drink;
Drink till I'm empty,
Drink till you're full,
Drink till you've forgotten
The rules of lives of cruel.

Then run.
Take this blood-filled cup;
And run.

Don't look back,
Run lightly enough
To leave no tracks,
And run.

I'll try to follow,
But my legs will break,
As I'm all too hollow.

Don't you worry,
Don't show your sympathy,
Just take this blood-filled cup,
Drink,
And run.

Bitten Tongue

He doesn't know what to write,
She doesn't know what to feel;
Insubordinate to his own will,
She's afraid of the concealed.

Revealed is what's known
To his lover he's shown,
But the hidden has wheeled

Something derailed,
Something off trail;
Leaving the supposed truth
So miserably frail,

And now her disguise has failed.
Labelled with a short fuse,
No longer easily amused,
Now too easily confused

For there are too many secrets
For any human to hold on to.
So mangled will the screw
Of deceit leave you,

So shamefully manipulated
Will these secrets claim your shoes
With a mind now ready to lose
To the numbers of few who

Accept the death they can't choose.
It'll end, as is the evident trend;
No longer could any man defend
A lover's life with too many lies to commend.

Stay Strong

You're weak and you're alone.
You haven't been here for very long,
Just stay a little strong
And you'll get past all that's wrong.
You just need a friend to phone.
Words of emptiness and loneliness
Have you consumed in this darkness,
But! You'll prevail with your cleverness.

Survive the Winter

And every time I shiver, I just remember:
All the times you would come closer
In order to keep me warmer.
I was not made for an everlasting winter;
So just once more, come closer.
Aid me to build this shelter
To fend off the killer shivers.

Support

Whisper to me
Your sorrowful words of death.
I'll respond to your self-pity;
"It ain't over yet
Your strength shall not be wrought.
With this candle,
I'll be your support."

Embrace Prisoner

A link to and old odd world;
It's so dark and full of abyssal swirls.
These swirls, the twirl effortlessly into my sight
Prior to vanishing before my wicked eyes.
And there they lie, yonder by my heart
To ponder what they sought to start.
A cleanup of their old scars
Parted by thunderous storms and sickly sparks.
My place of dreams awaits
With a welded gate that locks itself away.
From the rooms it uses to play,
The place I use to stay.

The one without claim.
The one that can't be touched.
No time to be maimed,
Bones can't be crushed.
Reach and gain
The heart that can't be tamed.
Bring forth the rain;
Wash the wounds in pain.
Undim the lights of trust.
Let flow, the blood of lust.
Plague the wicked crust
With the early stages of a loves must.
Closed doors lead to the insane.
Open the floodgates; to rush.
Drop all you feign.
Allow polishing of the rust.

Fur

Fur on my lip, as my breath barely slips.
Something unspoken yearns for a kiss.

Fur on my tongue, holding words unsung.
A broken song that would boom like a gun.

Fur in my mouth, an itching, and a drought,
Each strand a token of torment and doubt.

Fur from my lungs, coughing up black gunk,
Awaking; just a dream, a memory defunct.

Persona Identify

It's an evident fact that strength is something that I lack.
Under each breath, I crumble under my own back.
Cataloguing all my defeats, without blood on my hands,
I've lost society's respect, without strength to demand.

My name is one to forget. Who can trust a mind
Without past horrors, portraying nothing but mirrors?
If people wanted a reflection, they'd look at their own river.
Maybe that's why, when they look at me, they shiver.

Even I shiver when I look upon my own river, my mirror;
The reflection of myself and all that resides and dwells.
When I see me, I get confused; a reflection of a reflection,
As to who is who? I haven't any clue who to choose.

Efforts to let loose, be me, be true, often conclude
In different ways than my persona likes to elude,
Or avoid discomfort and other's structured views.
Perhaps the thing that I pursue, is to live life in solitude.

Paradigm Shift

Weld shut the gate of trust
As trust implies certainty;
Nothing is certain.
Draw open the theatre of statistics!
For a broken age
Demands a broken stage
Full of broken acts
Based on logical facts.

The Odd Key

A pole reversal on familiar feelings
Leaves playfulness and love
As foreign and strange things.
While it's possible, as I sit with you all,
A moment to laugh can easily be scored.
Unknowingly a bug tramples the halls
And brings the anxiety out of the walls.
Just as easily does one get mad
When the other slurs something sad.
Upon this do the bricks corrode
To a colour that brings back home.
And this familiarity is of what I speak.
An odd key to a place which I was raised.
Warped, sullen humour keeps happiness at reach.

The Dead Think of Shallow Pasts

I took it upon myself, not to dwell,
But to dive into a perspective of wealth
And modest health stealthily
Against a prior mindset sheltered
By a shroud of feathers, and silk that melts.

I died only to break the ruse,
My mind caved only to let the silk sift through;
Although now a single colour highlights my view.
But fear was an unexplored cave;
Now no longer is it so new,
And this shade, who knew?
This grey would be something to hold onto.

Not a scale anyone would likely choose
With so many greens and blues,
Rude reds and violent violet hues;
Now we're all equally queued,
We can sit next to each other on this pew.

Nothing of a religious sense, but instead,
A wedding to betroth differences and mend
Our fragile ideas of what was said, and when.
An epiphany of which I aim to tend.

But for now;
No den can hold us from our death,
No freedom can shelter us from our end,
No loneliness can hinder us from the trend
Of being one again with the soil we tread.

Passages passed and disintegrated;
So much time wasted.
My vessel had been dislocated
From its binds, its residence;
I wasn't in the right place back then.
Decapitated, through blood there was dread.
I had lost my wits, my head;
It was as if I were dead.
So many ill words tolerated;
So many a false pledge.
So much for actions consolidated;
So much do I regret.
Lured to reflect past an ever-blooming hedge
The fortune read, was naught but malevolence.

A Matter of Perspective

Silence

You're supposed to be quiet.
You will die in your silence!
With a cold scream,
Your voice barely breaks
The ink-filled dreams.

Writing off the pain,
Set it free, against the grain.
Then, to take its place
Another is unleashed;
A fury so uncanny.

What motivates your
Decline from the fountain
Of harmony? Whisper
Your sorrows no more,
The effort is worthless.

In the end, your words
Just sink right through
The floor. Just continue
Writing, that is your
Only endorsed chore.

Little do your demons
Know, that through your
Notes, you will scream
Louder than the infinite
Suffering of bones.

Recall, you are supposed
To be quiet, and you will die
In your silence, with a voice
Less than a whisper,
But with words of infinite
power.

Climb to Mars

The branches I climbed upon,
With vines that seemed so
strong,
As I ascended to a new world;
Yet, a world I was born from.
The branches and the vines
Began to crack, to snap, to
unwind;
Now I'm stuck, with no way
back,
And so, I weep under the stars,
I knew my home would always
be
Deep in the heart of Mars.

Moderation

Moderation is key, linger around
The charred and an ember will
Haunt your scars. Dedicate yourself
To yourself and no one else.

One can be an extension of you,
To this I suggest you choose
A moderate portion to consume,
A portion they submit for use.

The Balance

Yes, fill your mind with positivity,
But also take the time to reflect
On all that is negativity.
If one lacks a heart for reality,
Take peace in knowing it offers clarity.
There's no such thing as charity,
Everything pays a price; neutrality.
So, if you are to seek the good in things,
The price must be of dark maturity,
And an understanding of evil beings.

To Kill a Demon

To slay your undying demon,
To forever be in a perpetual state
Of ridding yourself from his vim
You must identify your worst traits;
The better it is that they be so grim.
Treats so wretched he shan't refuse a taste
So his head will bow for you to make a trim.

Night and Day

Now, that was a wonderful day; alas,
We must slide across the drapes.
Time for darkness, it falls like fate,
So beautiful, but easy to hate.

The time that we strive to sleep through,
The reality we strive to escape.
You've witnessed days' brightness,
Seen the meaning behind its hopefulness.

Time now to be placed in reality's distress.
Time now to undress the heart that you caress,
Leaving it exposed for the wickedness
To be digested, a haunting moment of evilness.

However, once day falls to night, never fear,
So shall night fall today; the time is near.
Another wonderful day awaits you dear,
As we spin again around our sphere.

Burn

Burn all that is non-constructive;
Burn,
Burn it all,
Burn.
Burn your anxieties,
Burn.
Burn your hate,
Burn.
Burn your anger,
Burn.
Burn your fears,
Burn.
Burn.
Burn it all,
Burn;
And take back your mind.

Close Despair

There is a darkness in each of us
That will only mutilate our lust,
Dwindling a delicate flux within
Our murder of a raven's crux.

We'd flock through stormy weather
And shed together, our feathers,
Exposing our melting tremors
That would otherwise indicate our tethers.

Forever in a feverish silence, never
To speak of our mindlessness.
Note a mote of delinquency,
Fickle be our innocence.

Run from the tongue of despair,
There's only evil dwelling in his lair.
Take as many paces from it as you can,
No longer hear its evil whisper in your ear.

Camp out there, where you can muster up
That courage, encrust your soul
With just enough trust to singe away
All those fears that you constantly hear.

They're a useless part of your fringe
That you sweep behind your ear
As you leer at false images in hopes
To quit the way you sear.

Else, burnt ashes is all you'll come near.
You have to peer out to the open world,
Embrace it and love it, for a new you to emerge.
It just make sense, to not dwell in your hurt.

My Lungs

Breath... breath...
Don't forget to breath.
My skin, wrapped in a cluster
Of blisters, as I near the killers.
You drop the pin into my lap,
Once again I am trapped.

Trapped... trapped...
I forgot to keep breathing.
Let some out, release.
Words flow with ease,
Gracefully. Blood is cooling,
The abyss, no longer consuming.

Poetry... poetry...
Allows me to breath,
I can finally breath.

A New Direction

Wouldn't it be nice if you had
You as a friend? But in spite
Of all your good work, mad
That you can only be polite
For so long, temporarily can hide
What dwells behind your eyes,
Trapped so deep inside,
A complete mystery lies.

You deserve a reward,
Not another epiphany;
Face the facts, you lie
In utter misery.
You only hold the ability
To grant advisory.
It's time for action;
While taking control
And maintain chivalry.

Climb out of your hole
And you will soon be
On a new journey,
In a new direction
Of infinite discovery;
And it will all end
So wonderfully.

Be Free

Trapped in the middle,
The game, such a riddle;
Heart thrown in a puddle.
The situation, too muddled,
Where do you go
To follow its flow?

You've been here for so long;
Under your feet, the weeds
Have grown and crumbled under
The weight of blood as you bleed.
The potential of flowers proceeds,
Be careful of the seeds

Planted in your chest,
They'll most likely sprout thorns
For your selfish needs.
Unwilling to release
What once set you free,
Ironically, it now holds

You captive against
Your wails and pleas.
Rip yourself from this teat,
The nutrients gained,
Are not what you seek.

There is more to this game
Than what you can see;
You're destined for fame,
For nothing but glory.

Put your heart elsewhere,
And to good use,
They will give you glares,
But to be honest,
Do you really care?

You've lost all your hair
Due to the stress,
Seems so unfair.
You shouldn't be here,

You deserve to be there;
A place where no one stares.
Uproot your planted feet,
And walk, walk, walk
Away from this pitiful talk.
Walk away, run if you must.

Stray from the path
If you wish, this life
Is yours; not owned by
A sweet kiss.
You're not running,
Never, will you flee.

All you're doing
Is setting yourself free;
You're fighting back,
And there's not really
A damn thing
Wrong with that.

Broken Stones

Ignorance brings us to quits,
But if you take the hits,
You'll then see that with
The walls being broken,
You'll learn to replace
One brick with six.

Twitch, with a switch
To intermit in the shift;
You've allowed room
For a pure kiss.
The truth is 'that' luxurious,
This comes as a promise.

I may behold a heart
That remains homeless,
But this heart of mine
Is also still so cautious.
It's learnt a lot from
Wondering in loneliness.

Without a directed gaze,
I've acquired the ability
To see benevolently.
Where it previously
Did not exist, between
Trees, that the average eye
Can only see as mist.

Between the nodes,
Are all fractured bones
Of those who'd failed
To make the distance thrown.
With effort, we can pick up
The right flailing stone.

By the end of the road,
After a long journey,
Our health begins to corrode.
At the end of the road
You 'will' have something
To tell and show.

Break the Chains

She's afraid of hurting him
More than she already has.
She's afraid of hurting him
By being a broken burden.
She's afraid of hurting him
By not returning emotion.
She's afraid of hurting him;
She's simply… afraid.

He hates the pain
She's put him in.
He hates the pain
She couldn't prevent.
He hates the pain
That broke his defence.
He hates the pain;
He simply… hates.

Don't be afraid
To face the flames,
For, you are the water
To calm their fury.
Don't hate the gate
That locks your needs
Away in place, for fear
Is often the strongest lock.

Fear can be broken
Only by denial;
Hate can be soothed
Only by acceptance of trials.
Look at each other,
Gaze upon the other's eyes.

Whisper solemnly
To each other,
"We must, in
Each other, place
Our everlasting faith."
We'll be alright,
We'll win this game,
As long as we can
Break these chains.

Broken Dreams

A list I see of a twisted heap of broken dreams,
Dreaming peacefully, only then, does one gleam.
The only place we can be set free. Leaning on this tree,
A habit others will keep, no opportunity to take a leap.

Seeping their way deeper away from truly being set free;
Eventually, they meet the creep that hides beneath.
See to it they run, find what they truly need,
But intimidated, and directed back by a fake gun;

Countered with a lunge;
All that is needed to make that plastic crunch.
You have a hunch that you can't take a punch;
Little do you know that you can do what you want.

Don't let yourself be shunned by others hurtful taunts,
Don't be bothered by just a bunch of runts;
That's what they want, it's what they hunt;
You can burn brighter than their shallow sun.

Cadmean Victory

Surveying the aftermath, I find
No room left to bury alive
The most vengeful of the hive.
By knowing I could be wiser
Ensuring in the end, I'm a survivor.

Monsters made of mirrors,
And ravenous shadowed killers,
Were spawned by a broken perspective
And fought memories harshly neglected.
Amidst this battlefield I witnessed
What happens when darkness enters.

A sigh of relief displays the least
Of our renowned skies.
So to say with peace,
I was broken only
By nothing but a good fight.

Connected

To bring about a smile,
To bring about a frown;
What strings to beguile,
Or what heads to crown?

You can find this pattern
Somewhere dark, or somewhere light.
But you can find it only
Deep inside your mind's eye.

Dive deep and endless.
Wander nowhere through the mist.
Each stroke, brings clairvoyance;
Each step, brings a relaxed fist.

Corrosive Bliss

Drink upon this acid flask,
Play upon this magic harp
And look upon the contrast.
A taste so bitter,
So corrosive to the touch;
But a sound of vigour,
So simpler than the rough.
To comprehend her surge
You would first
Have to render your urge.
Purge the mind
Of sinister turn
As it's easy to experience hurt,
And to have the acid
Leave you burnt.
So, strive only
For her bliss and her beauty.
Look past the unruly;
Listen to her soft harmony,
The golden melody
Of everlasting clarity,
Till finally
The reward for the effort
Will almost look like charity.

Dauntless

Conjured far from your homeland shores,
While protected by good thoughts and serendipity,
Is a storm that feeds on any oppressive thought
And is lured by the scent of your melancholy.
Its arrival is inevitable,
From the moment
You had
A thought…
When it comes,
You must weather the storm.

Water drawn from the deepest depths of the ocean
Spouts about with torrential force,
The storm has arrived.
You must weather the storm.

And what if the storm never passes?
Weather it some more.
Should it never cease?
Embrace it,
Embrace it and love it.
You can become it, sure.
And in doing so, no matter where you tread,
Never will you ever feel the rain again.

The Road

As we walk down this road in the absence of light,
Our souls are constantly struggling in an endless fight.
And although it's as hard and as harsh as loneliness can be,
We will push on, and put our demons to their knees.

In the midst of the darkness
Where there's an intensity of tears,
A newfound strength will stop this
As a new you appears.

Pay No Mind

'Tis only a feather,
But I'm so obsessive, I'd better
Be tethered to a letter
Authored by a heart that sputters
And murmurs, and records its mutters.
A letter that would be addressed
To my mindless obeisance
Of things that rarely impress,
Of things so commonly missed;
Yet, I bind to this feather
Something so worthless
Alone;
Like a stone
To a mountain
That towers,
A piece
Of something
Greater,
A reminder
To ponder...
I wonder...
No...
'Tis
Only
A fea-
the-
r.

Defeated Demon

I know what you are,
The darkness to my star.
Yes, I know what you are,
The abyss that hands me scars.

You and I share a past,
And you've shown me life is hard,
But this is where I get harsh
And turn your land to marsh.

Solid ground was swept out
From underneath of you.
In my mind, there is no room
For my conflict with the Gloom.

I know the reality,
I know the truth,
So now I come through,
And show you the ruse.

In having defeated
This horrorsome demon,
I have now chosen
A better illumination.

I know what you are,
The entity of my star.
Yes, I know what you are,
The bliss to heal my scars.

Escape and Follow

A weak link
Shrinks and sinks
Away from the brink
Of destruction; retreats.
Greet a new dawn,
Bite down on it.
If you break your teeth,
It's a sign that
Your hard work
Is not yet in decline.
Melodic chimes are
Luring you to what
Is right. Follow,
And you'll be fine.
Wipe away the grime,
There's still so much time,
Bring yourself some pride,
Don't rush it all in a
Single fall of night.
The bright of day
Must always follow
When darkness comes.
"There is a light
At the end of the tunnel,"
We say, for everyone.

Pressure

On the outside you're bright!
On the inside resides
'Something' that lies.
What drives, and pries,
In your sorrow filled mind?
In your silence, crying,
Over societies science?
Pressured by the sightless,
Giving you reminders
On why to feel hopeless.

However, never you fret,
The pressure won't last
Forever, you'll be okay,
Learn from your past,
Come out of this ever
More the wiser,
The stronger you'll be
Once you can sever
The demons that lurk
To feed on your hurt.

Empathy: Part Two

A burning light sparks as I
Notice your laugh.
You're drowned
In others mud,
But still
Are able to suck it up,
Continue through the rough.
You're an inspiration,
A reason to get by,
To breathe through my
Affliction. Your smile
Breaks the wretched,
And seeing you happy
Is a gift for those
Left so fractured.

Depression is a disease, and your happiness is
The cure. Putting my pain to ease I'm baited
By your benevolent lure, and I want nothing
Other than to feel the presence of your
Aura. I sometimes feel that empathy is a curse,
But then you remind me, through being able to see
What you see, empathy; is one of the greatest gifts
You can receive.

Eternal

There is no beginning, there is no end.
Like a dream, it seems, we are placed in
The middle to form our own trend.
Our minds and bodies will rise, will fall,
But our souls are vitalised. Eternal,
They will never halt, as all of this
Is an endless hall. We will discover
New rooms; some big, some small,
Some so cruel they'll bend us to a crawl.
Nothing can stop us, no, nothing at all.
We have been given the kiss, the call,
That lends us the strength to brawl.

Remain Content

At the pinnacle of bliss,
Hold your good intentions,
And keep your benevolence
As it is, to maintain happiness;
To keep it as you so wish.
Brilliance can be any
Beauty you perceive.
Believe there's good
Will still to receive,
And the Earth's song
Will sing to you
Its heart felt dream.
If love does not exist,
We wouldn't have known
Of its existence.
You're looking at
The wrong pictures,
If you feel this pestilence.

Truth

Can you hear it?
Echoing between emptiness, effortlessly.
A hypnotic chime pulses carelessly;
The bells thrive when all's silent.
The truth rings a rhythm; enlightened.
Let it linger.

Can you feel it?
A foreign pressure in the dry breeze.
When the air is still, still depth is seized.
Its demands prevail when all's lost;
The truth binds, but unbinding is the cost.
Submit to its influence.

Tranquilizer

Rise and fall, and between, endure the grind
That ensures I can fall safely each night.
A grind, driven by a purpose to rise each time.
When purpose and fire begin to wane and die
A poem a day unravels the spirit, to summarise.

The more powerful the purpose is trained,
The intensity of the abyss follows its way
Through jagged paths and trees that sway.
Again as nighttime falls my mind's made prey,
But a poem a day keeps the nightmare at bay.

Wake and abolish the torments so horrid,
By remembering a purpose so flourished.
This is a natural process we have all harnessed
And garnered prosperity by purpose so pampered.
With the vision of you, I've remained untarnished.

Keep up the momentum from rising I've gained,
From forgetting miseries, and in their blank space
Cast down and bury the demons I've since slain.
Slain by my viciousness now needing more play;
But a touch from you keeps the beast tamed.

Universe

Its emptiness is filled
With anything and everything,
Even nothing consists of something,
As nothing is something.

The empty set, is a set in itself,
Baring nothing, and nothing is something.
And something can't be nothing.

Everything is something
Nothing doesn't exist
Much like our imagination, the universe is endless
    Maybe.
More so, of riddles, than answers;
But it can all be answered…

          … Maybe…

Spread thin
    And sporadic
      The universe   likes   to   be   dramatic.

Look up entropy, it's obvious.
Look up black holes, star clusters, and galaxies.
Look at how profound it all really is,
In this giant particle salad.

Sun

The Sun, and its repeating,
Perpetual ignitions, with
Dramatic effects as explosive
As its own cyclic explosions.

Along with mass particle
Ejection for our nutrition,
Are in part, what retains
Its famous recognition.

Never, will it devolve to
A red giant in my time set,
Nor yours, or your next,
Or your next's next, next…

Next.

Neither will it become
A white dwarf, extinguished,
Until after Andromeda
Inevitably hits us.

Assuming it stays
Out of the firing line,
Which it likely will,
In that oncoming miracle.

Scorching storms and
Tornadoes of fire,
Flares that breach
Atmospheres higher;

So chaotic and destructive;
I can think of nothing finer.
The light that gives us life,
That could never be brighter.

A Matter of Perspective

Moon

Beyond twilight, when all is dark
And no sunshine,
An otherwise masked figure
Takes the Sun's residual glow
To illuminate our otherwise
Pitch-black midnight sky.

The presence the Sun gives it,
Passes gracefully slow
And our perception's branded
By cycling phases of the night.
For some, it captivates and
Engages their emotional growth;

Ultimately, for all, it activates
Oceans to shift with the tide.
The Moon influences our Earth
By coasting while apart.

Even to bask in its luminance
Can soothe a tired, weary soul;
It's no wonder our closest celestial body
Inspires symbolism in art,
Or portrays a sentient entity,
Like a character made whole.
Its Lunar presence presents us
A spectacular, pearly heart,
And with it, a different taste
Of a moon-lit life to stroll.
With the Moon keeping watch,
Dare you be afraid of the dark?

Earth

Bound and bogged, we're rotating along.
Centripetal forces reverberate gravity's silent song.
A lifestyle here, on our 'roughly-spherical,' sapphire planet,
Alters and changes; we can live as total polar opposites,
Depending directionally on where our nearest pole is.

The Earth provides only what we can take.
When we can't, we outsmart before changing place.

Seek an expansive forest,
Luscious with all sorts of colours,
Or shades of grey, concrete jungles,
Where it's only money that matters.
A serene lifestyle can await you,
With all conflict peacefully answered;
We got it all.

Alternatively, you can seek out
Our many fine violent establishments.
Opportunities to become wealthy,
Or lack thereof in poorer conditions.
It is a privilege to call shots;
Although options still exist in oppression.
We got it all.

Experience things so soft and beautiful.
There's also hideous and rough!
Live gloriously in the light or hidden away in the dark.
Be attracted. Be repulsed. What makes you laugh?
Good. Bad. Nothing more.
We got it all.

A Matter of Perspective

And through it all that we have
We have at least one another
Within our Earth and all its splendour.
You can find it all.

Life and death are met in equal force,
But only in life can it be explored.
Through the darkest nights
And brightest of days,
The Earth gives it all.

Nature

Not a single thing could better encapsulate
    A drive so primal,
Than observing any of our Earthly creatures
    Thrive; as entitled.
Removing cognition exposes a natural state
    So emotional,
So honest, so completely and utterly unbiased.

Aside from basing its influence
    From sheer, unwavering survival;
Aside from instinctively aiding nature
    To blossom and flourish.
I was stunned to learn, to experience
    That a life beyond survival exists.
The creatures that are our neighbours,
    Playing, exploring;
So many other things betwixt.

Living to survive isn't at all,
    All that matters.
I was stunned to learn, to experience that a life
    Can provide beyond
Its own measure. Working with synergy to
    Unbind from stagnation,
From a shackled life unfulfilled
    By Earth's splendour,
In another of nature's spawned creations.

Its influence can be as dramatic as a
    Warning of predators,
Or as small, yet impactful, as carrying pollen
    From tree to tree.
Nothing better represents a persistence
    In presence
Than admiring plants, taking up every spot
    Of residence,
In every nook and cranny of this Earth we Inhabit.

Our local plant life grows with such resilience,
    Entirely unphased
Holding no judgment toward our daily goings
    And dramatizations
Yet asserts itself as required, for all life to be
    Triumphant.
I was stunned to learn, to experience the infinite form,
    Plant life gives
In numbers to fit between all our levels of artificial layers.

How effortlessly it can overrun a now dilapidated memory
    Of existence.
I was stunned to learn, to experience how everything is
    So connected,
And tied, but not confined by, plants and their innate ability
    To give Oxygen and nutrients.
Its influence can be as dramatic as hindering a tsunami,
    Or as small,
Yet as impactful, as giving bees a purpose.

Human

Me, myself, and I;
Mind, body, and soul.

The mind alive and writhing
In the unknown;
It's unwise and untested
Until independent.

Selfishly selfless, and oh
So wickedly reckless;
Trials begin blind,
With naught to reference.

Structured destruction
Remains equidistant
From beginning and end;
Both are so elusive.

The mind alive and
Yearning the known.
It could have been
Anything, any vessel,

A body shimmering
Shapeless until shaped
By sculptors, neither
Benign nor estranged

Some of which, so
Romantically drape,
Pluck, and peel,
With nothing left fettered.

Paradoxical to ideals,
A body is restrained.
In matter alone,
It doesn't matter;

Only a vessel.
Everything shapes
The flow of our souls
Into each, these fragile

Leaking canvases.
It pours, and it purrs,
And it often ravages.
A consciousness is defined

By its limits; just tools, fidgets,
Delicately bridging bridges,
And bridges. The flow
Of our soul's shape everything;

Mind, body, and soul;
Me, myself, and I.

Give Everything

All that I have, I give…

To her, wanting her to be strong.
I couldn't desire more,
Than to prevent her being me,
And to raise her to be strong,
Learning from her weaknesses.
In certain moments, she will be weak,
She may experience this harshly.

To teach her what I've learnt,
Not just as a base itself,
For, I do not wish her strength
To be stretched to such lengths;
The way I learnt to traverse,
That left a foul and bitter taste.

To show her it's always okay to cry;
No matter of sight, tactically,
When it's time to hide internal fights,
That will likely last for her whole life.
I will show her how to hold a sword,
Her muscles protesting in strife;
Moments in movement must be concise!

To imbibe into her, a dauntless stoicism
Amidst schisms of shifting perspectives,
Being self-reflective for inner peace,
Growing insight into her inner beast.

To see her beam with glee,
Even when it's raining,
Or to be downcast when
The rains are waning.

To help her to defend
All that she holds above
This eternal blending
Of the give and take of love.

To her as a precious gift;
All that I could wish
Is from death to birth,
She learns her self-worth.

Perspective

I never noticed that star before…

A great perspective is never granted,
Only earned. So elusive, but of great worth.
It was far too easy to resist and reject
A great perspective that knew me best.
So, I learned; the easier the perspective,
The perspective is for worse.
But it could be worse; I learnt.

Arcturus, it goes by Arcturus…

How can you reject what's made.
What's made permanent stays.
Scars in the mind, they prey,
I learned, on stars portrayed
And splashed away to fade.

Arcturus. It's so bright…

I reject and detest! Nothing knows
Me best, not like the darkness.
Why fight? Beasts can be pets.
No light, yet no rest; I didn't learn!

But Arcturus sure is burning brightly tonight…

An abrupt epiphany suddenly reveals a truth
So honest, one that dissolves, the moment
It acknowledges, anything that questions
It as being anything other than perfect.
A great perspective could make me
A detective, forensically piecing
the narrative as it should best fit.
I could learn. So, I learned

The Gloom promises nothing frightening,
Not when I'm familiar now, with all that
Lurks within. Lucidity promises nothing
Welcoming, not even when in daylight
Can crimes be so grim. I learned everything
Can be found everywhere. What you see
Is what you think, nothing is bare.

It's all just a matter of perspective;

Arcturus burns brightly every night.

The Blooming

Part 1

I wander a field of broken glass.
Each step a grind, none shall be my last.

All horrors are forgettable,
Even the treachery, though immeasurable,
Passes as nothing but normal;
One becomes blissfully miserable.
The Suffering is impenetrable.

I wander contorted and alone.
Amidst the glass, black vision is sewn.

With everything in view
Swallowed by a darkened hue,
It all became so skewed.
It's true, you can't know the gloom
Without a glow to hold on to.
No light? No gloom.
It all became nothing;
The Suffering is subdued.

I wander and wonder, ponderings
Naught to remember; glass reminders.

Behold before my lonely path,
A crimson pillar so similar,
Yet unfamiliar to the totems
I left behind me far.

I was sure I was alone in my endeavours,
Yet a crimson pillar
Be a semblance of something other.
I am like no other,
Yet there is another.
The Suffering may falter.

I wonder and reminisce about a time
Before broken glass, when all was bliss.

Though memories have faded,
And my body broken and contorted,
A pulse has penetrated and thwarted
This darkness; I was enshrouded.
The pulse purposefully emanated
From this singular ornament
That seems so differently created.
My pillars were sacrificial,
And left me disheartened, to offer

Shade at the cost of becoming wretched;
This structure was constructed
To puncture the dead and darkened.
Could it be it was made to make
An inner one's inner-self hardened
And keep them well hidden?
The Suffering seems centred.

I wonder, in a field of broken glass,
Each thought to reflect on all that passed.
A rhythmic pulse is persisting,
Reverberating a response
To my faintest heart beating.

Although the pulse fleeting
Appears not from this finding;
I'm observing it to be originating
Delicately from what exists within;
A crystalline being abiding,
Residing in this crystalised encasing.
A spark within my darkened heart
Conjured an enlightening epiphany,
Establishing the pulsing as a signal
Of another soul, still somewhat living.
The suffering is retreating.

I wonder severance of broken glass,
And relevant benevolence.

Part 2

What a wonder and joy
To employ upon such a simple,
Observational exploit!
I glanced upon a shimmer
Annoyed by the presence of my
Coy finger upon this crimson buoy.

All the while, a pulsing
Ameliorates its noise,
The shapeless, shimmering decoy
Is destroyed, as it ripples into
A feminine figure, with a gaze
That nurtures my inner boy.

And where my finger had caressed
The rigidity of this crimson pillar
Ceases and becomes a pliable putty.

Ahoy! Curiosity stirs within me
As I toy imaginings to remould
This crimson clay into a shape
Fit only for if consent is deployed,
Should our unknown figure desist
Entirely its structure and poise.
A blooming I mustn't avoid.

I apply mind to wield
In a field of broken glass,
Hope in time is mine.
All it took was a single wink,
A signal to declare
An envisioned eternal link.

A unanimous decision to sync in unison
And produce an optimal image in which,
On glimpse, one would dare not blink.
The suffering's destruction is on the brink

As I push down on this pillar, causing it to shrink.
With a pull, it stretches to my peak,
And from this, I fathom its limits and kinks.

The woman in crimson watches
With approval and submission,
The final decision to beckon our vision,
So enlightened, into a tangible composition.
A convulsion of movements commission
The pillar to refine and define the
Optimal figure, growing and contorting
Into a lone work of forestation.

A Matter of Perspective

In a flash, a tree, with branches and leaves,
Each adding their own beautification.
Such a wonderful sight before my decrepit eyes,
Which forces a new motivation.
My loss came in two, and I
Am one tree short, it's clear how
I must clear prior trepidation.
A blooming calls inspiration.

I apply mind to create within broken glass,
Where two trees must take shape.
A tree that stands so sincere,
Company it must have; a fact so clear.
Sheer likeness beside it,
A reality so near.

Part 3

My feet become planted into the glass,
As a hollow heart in me sears, yearning to be
A compliment of a sweet tree.

Roots shoot forth here, from below my scarred feet.
The severe fear from a torment passed, disappears
From memories; now mere specks in bloodied, rolling tears.

Finally, the fire in me spears-forth in queer
Form, from my body: blasting, smearing
A bloody mist across the ambient atmosphere.

Where the grim and austere mist falls,
A bed of grass sprouts, geared
For a restful and calm career.

A blooming only I can hear.
I apply mind for no mind;
Forever, to the suffering I am blind.

It could have almost gone unnoticed,
A twig that found its solace
Amidst a bed of modest, softened grass.

A twig, a fragment, to be something significant.
No conscious thought would assume its sentience;
No prescience, two trees would be in human presence.

A blooming of life's essence.
The suffering served a purpose.
But the cost…

Was worth everything.

Burn this book!

Other published work:

The World in Our Words – Published in 2024, this collaborative anthology of poems was written by twenty-two poets from around the world. Organised by Stephannie Rowe, this book consists of poems that describe the world as each poet sees it from their corner of the world. It is a true masterpiece of what art can look like when so many people put aside their differences, their opinions, and focus on a singular goal and purpose. In this collection, each poet was allowed to submit up to six pieces of poetry; although with the kindness of Stephannie Rowe, Nate was allowed to enter seven.

Thanks Steph!

Work in progress:

A yet-to-be titled collection of short stories which are a slightly grim in nature. One of which involves a were-spider, and another about a man dropping a grenade in his bath instead of a bath bomb.

A yet-to-be-titled book set in a fantasy world revolving around elves specifically. In this world, infants are tossed straight out of the city and deep into the forest where they must learn how to live and survive without even knowing how to talk or... walk. Eventually when they come of age, they can re-enter the city to train academically... Except, they still don't know how to talk let alone read.

Pinball Dictates – A story set in a world where everything is settled with Pinball. The goal with this story is to eventually turn it into a video game. Maybe some more poetry... One day.

About the Author...

Or more so about his writing journey:

Nate has always enjoyed writing since learning how to write. It was always preferred over other art forms as he felt he had the most control over getting his ideas out into 'something'; unlike, for example, drawing. It was always possible to describe every single detail with more words, than it was to get detail with more pencil strokes. Nate always found words interesting, always eager to find the meaning of new and unknown words and different ways to manipulate their meaning with different context.

As Nate went through his school years, English would always be the favourite subject. And the most enjoyable projects in other subjects were ones that he could use his writing skills in some way. Although the desire to attend school gradually faded as a certain darkness crept in toward the end of his school years, so too, did his desire to write. Until...

Until an attempt to create a piece of writing in the likeness of something he would hear in an Eminem song was made. Something about the rhymes, and finding a rhythm, and the expressiveness in the words that were directly reflective of what he was feeling; made him want to do it again. And again. And over the years, when a release was needed, release was found in the writing of a poem.

Nate's poetry started in the form of a lyrically intensive song, but as time passed, a style more consistent with traditional poetry was formed. Bad things could sound like good things, and in turn he learnt how to make good things sound like bad things. The depth of interpretive language made itself known, along with how to pace the reader, and so Nate conformed with a style that broke certain standards but was true to what his intention with a poem was.

A style that meant one thing to one reader, and another to another reader. Highly interpretable with strong use of imagery, heavy focus on rhythm, heavier focus on rhyme.

The journey of learning his own identity in poetry, stayed while other aspects of life rose and fell. Nate dropped out of school. Got a job. Started a family. Toward the forming of a family, the writing started to slip away as things got better. Poetry as a release was becoming less required. And writing in general, not just poetry, was being forgotten in place of the new obsession.

Now: Nate has reconciled with his love of writing and realised its place isn't just one for release when things aren't so great, but as a method to show appreciation. Or simply for the love of creation. He has nurtured this love of writing and taken it more seriously, after all, art is sometimes all that's left of one's legacy and place in the world. And who can fight the request of those fans who crave more?

Nate will write on.

… Oh, you wanted to know about Nate's life? Where the darkness came from? What specifically did Nate go through that made things good again? I don't know, I only work here. Maybe Nate will write an autobiography one day…